The Life and Ministry of Jesus' 12 Disciples

The Twelve Disciples

Peter

James

John

Andrew

Philip

Bartholomew

Matthew

Thomas

James

Thaddaeus

Simon the Zealot

Judas Iscariot

GENERAL INFORMATION • PERSONALITY AND CHARACTER
ENCOUNTERS WITH JESUS • SCRIPTURE REFERENCES
KEY LESSONS • STORIES

ROSE PUBLISHING

Who are the Twelve Disciples?

Their Backgrounds

- The twelve disciples were from the Galilee region except for Judas Iscariot, who was from Judea.
- Their occupations ranged from fisherman to tax collectors and revolutionaries.
- Some were married. (see Mark 1:29-31; 1 Corinthians 9:3-6)
- Some were well-versed in Scripture. (see John 1:46)

Their Purpose

- After being baptized by John the Baptist and spending 40 days in the wilderness, Jesus started teaching and many people started following him.
- After a night of prayer and meditation, Jesus chose twelve men out of all those who were following him.
- These twelve men would be Jesus' main focus of instruction.
- These disciples were selected to let the world know of God's love, that God sent Jesus to redeem the world. (see John 17:23)

Their Mission

- These are the twelve men who, for the most part, would prove to be valuable companions to Jesus.
- Their instruction and conversations would become the teachings, knowledge, and instruction for the church that would later grow and spread.
- Jesus knew their personalities, both strong and weak.
- Jesus knew that these men would disappoint him, desert him, deny him, and betray him.
- Jesus knew that these men, once filled with the Holy Spirit, would be the first witnesses of the Gospel, carrying God's message of redemption to Judea, Samaria, and the ends of the earth.
- The twelve tribes of Israel were blessed in order to be a blessing to all nations. In a similar way, these twelve men, along with all disciples of Jesus who follow their lead, were to bless all nations. (see Galatians 3:8) Followers of Christ are commanded to go out and make disciples of all nations, baptizing them in the name of the Father, The Son, and the Holy Spirit.

Peter

- Simeon bar Jona (Simon, son of Jona)
- Cephas ("rock" or "a stone")
- Simon Peter
- Simon

- Son of Jona and born in Bethsaida.(John 1:42-44)
- Lived in Capernaum. (Matthew 8:5-14)
- Fisherman. (Matthew 4:18)
- Brother of Andrew. (Matthew 4:18)
- Partner with James and John.(Luke 5:10)
- Married. (Matthew 8:14)
- One of the pillars of the Jerusalem church. (Galatians 2:9)
- Boldly preached, healed, and ministered to Jews and Gentiles after Pentecost. (Acts 2–12)
- Imprisoned by Herod for preaching and rescued by an angel of the Lord. (Acts 12:3-19)
- Wrote 1 and 2 Peter.

- Impulsive (Matthew 14:28), yet cowardly. (Matthew 14:30; 26:69-74)
- Hot tempered (John 18:10), yet tenderhearted. (Matthew 26:75)
- Insightful (Matthew 16:16), yet dense. (Matthew 16:21-23)
- Courageous and solid after Pentecost. (Acts 5:27-30)

- Was called to be a fisher of men. (Matthew 4:19) Left everything to follow Jesus. (Luke 5:11)
- One of the three disciples in the core group of disciples. (Mark 5:37; 9:2; 13:3; 14:33)
- Simon said Jesus is the Christ, Son of the living God. Jesus names him Peter (rock) and said, "Upon this rock I will build my church, and the gates of Hell will not prevail against it." (Matthew 16:16-19)
- Was reprimanded because he refused to accept that Jesus had to die. (Matthew 16:23)
- Witnessed Jesus' Transfiguration (where Jesus' divinity was revealed). (Mark 9:2-8)
- Was sent to prepare the upper room for the Last Supper.(Luke 22:8)
- Jesus predicted that Peter would deny knowing him three times. (Luke 22:31-34)
- Was with Jesus in the Garden of Gethsemane. (Matthew 26:36-46)
- Jesus instructed Peter after his resurrection. (John 21:15-19)

God can forgive sins and strengthen the faith of those who love him.

Papias (second-century Christian) recorded that Mark served as Peter's scribe and wrote the Gospel of Mark based on Peter's testimony.
According to some stories, Peter asked to be crucified upside down.
Peter may have been crucified during the reign of Nero in Rome.
Symbols for Peter are sometimes keys, representing the keys to the kingdom of heaven. (Matthew 16:19)

Simon the Zealot

- Simon the Cananaean

- Was a Zealot. (Matthew 10:4; Mark 3:18; Luke 6:15; Acts 1:13)
- Listed as one of Christ's twelve disciples. (Matthew 10:2-4; Acts 1:13)
- The name Simon derives from the Hebrew name Shimon, meaning "hearing."
- The word "Cananaean" derives from an Aramaic word meaning "zealous one."

- Patriotic. (Matthew 10:4)
- Loyal. (Mark 3:18)
- Passionate. (Luke 6:15)
- Sacrificial. (Acts 1:13)

- Selected as one of Christ's twelve disciples. (Matthew 10:2-4; Acts 1:13)
- Sent out on a mission to the Jews to preach "the kingdom of heaven is at hand," heal the sick, cleanse the lepers, raise the dead, and cast out demons. (Matthew 10:5-8)
- Was present at the Last Supper. (Matthew 26:20)
- Was present for the Great Commission and Jesus' Ascension into heaven. (Matthew 28:16)

One should be willing to sacrifice his or her politics to follow Jesus.

One story suggests that Simon was the bridegroom at the wedding in Cana.

Some stories suggest that Simon was a missionary to Persia.

The symbol for Simon is sometimes a fish resting on a book, which is a reference to Simon fishing for people.

Judas Iscariot

- "Judas the Betrayer"
- Judas the son of Simon

- Judas was the treasurer for the group of disciples; was a thief. (John 12:5, 6; 13:29)
- Judas betrayed Jesus, felt remorse, threw the blood money in the temple and hanged himself. The chief priest used the money to purchase the potter's field, fulfilling prophecy. (Matthew 27:3-10)
- Judas purchased the Field of Blood and fell headlong and "burst open…" (Acts 1:18-20)
- Judas was replaced by Matthias who was added to the eleven apostles. (Acts 1:26)

- Greedy. (Matthew 26:14-16)
- Deceitful. (Matthew 26:25)
- Treacherous. (Matthew 26:47-50)
- Remorseful. (Matthew 27:3-5)

- Selected as one of Christ's twelve disciples. (Matthew 10:4; Luke 6:16)
- Jesus referred to Judas as the devil. (John 6:70, 71)
- Criticized Mary for anointing Jesus with expensive perfume. (John 12:4-8)
- Conversed with Jesus during the Last Supper. (Matthew 26:23-25; John 13:27, 28)
- The devil entered his heart at the Last Supper. (John 13:2)
- Betrayed Jesus for 30 pieces of silver. (Matthew 26:14-16; 47-51)

Not all who claim to follow Jesus are faithful to him and his goals.

Judas was possibly from Kerioth in Judea.

Some scholars suggest that Judas was a member of the Zealot sect known as the Sicarii, who were dagger-bearing assassins.

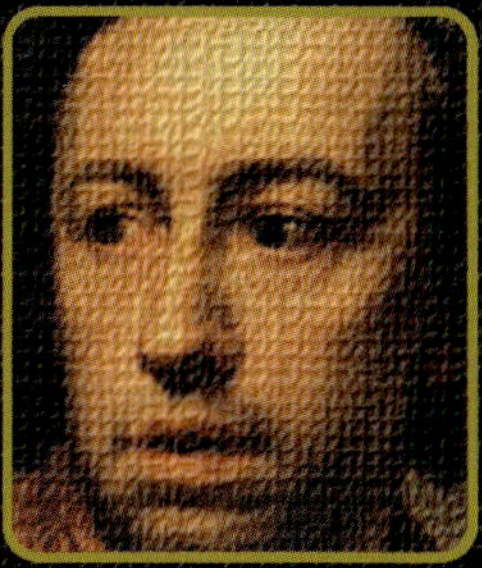

James, son of Alphaeus

- James the son of Alphaeus
- "James the Younger"
- "James the Less"

- Son of Alphaeus. (Mark 3:18)
- Possible brother of Matthew (Levi) the tax collector, also the son of Alphaeus. (Mark 2:14)
- Listed as one of Christ's twelve disciples. (Matt. 10:3; Acts 1:13)
- James the son of Alphaeus is often confused with James the brother of Jesus (who wrote the book of James) or James the brother of John.

- Unknown.

- Selected as one of Christ's twelve disciples. (Matthew 10:2-4; Luke 6:14-16)
- Sent out on a mission to the Jews to preach "the kingdom of heaven is at hand," heal the sick, cleanse the lepers, raise the dead, and cast out demons. (Matthew 10:5-8)
- Was present at the Last Supper. (Matthew 26:20)
- Was present when Jesus appeared to the disciples after the Resurrection. (John 20:19-25)

All followers of Jesus can still accomplish the work of God without being in the limelight.

Some suggest that James, son of Alphaeus, belonged to the revolutionary group known as the Zealots.
Tradition suggests that James was crucified in the Sinai or in Persia, or stoned to death in Jerusalem.

Thaddaeus

- Jude
- Judas the son of James
- Lebbaeus

- Son of James. (Luke 6:16)
- Listed as one of Christ's twelve disciples. (Matthew 10:2-4; Acts 1:13)
- The Aramaic meaning of both Thaddaeus and Lebbaeus is the same, "beloved" or "dear to the heart."
- The name "Judas" derives from the Hebrew name Judah, meaning "praise."
- Jude is sometimes confused with Judas the brother of Jesus, Judas Barsabbas, and Judas Iscariot.

- Inquisitive. (John 14:22)
- Confused. (John 14:22)

- Selected as one of Christ's twelve disciples. (Matthew 10:2-4; Acts 1:13)
- Sent out on a mission to the Jews to preach "the kingdom of heaven is at hand," heal the sick, cleanse the lepers, raise the dead, and cast out demons. (Matthew 10:5-8)
- Asked Jesus how he would reveal himself to his followers and not to the world. (John 14:22)
- Was present at the Last Supper. (Matthew 26:20)

Jesus will reveal his truths to believers who follow him.

Some suggest that Thaddaeus belonged to the revolutionary group, the Zealots.
Some scholars believe that Thaddaeus authored the book of Jude, although most believe the author is Judas, the brother of Jesus.
The symbol for Thaddaeus is sometimes a gold ship with silver sails before a red horizon, which is a reference to the ship he took on missionary journeys.

James, son of Zebedee

- Son of Zebedee
- Boanerges (Son of Thunder)
- "James the Elder"
- "James the Great"

- Son of Zebedee. (Matthew 4:21)
- Son of Salome. (Matthew 27:56; Mark 16:1)
- Fisherman with his father and his brother. (Matthew 4:18-22)
- Brother of John. (Matthew 4:21)
- Partner with Peter. (Luke 5:10)
- One of the pillars of the Jerusalem church. (Galatians 2:9)
- Put to death by the sword by Herod Agrippa I. The only one of the twelve disciples whose death for his faith was recorded in Scripture. (Acts 12:2)

- Vengeful and fiery. (Luke 9:54)
- Selfish and conceited. (Mark 10:35-37)
- Committed to Christ and courageous to the end. (Acts12:2)

- Was called to be a fisher of men. (Matthew 4:19) Left everything to follow Jesus. (Luke 5:11)
- One of the three disciples in the core group of disciples. (Mark 5:37; 9:2; 13:3; 14:33)
- Jesus named him and John "Sons of Thunder." (Mark 3:17)
- Was rebuked with his brother John for requesting God to rain fire on a Samaritan village. (Luke 9:54, 55)
- Witnessed Jesus' Transfiguration (where Jesus' divinity was revealed).(Mark 9:2-8)
- Jesus responded to James's and John's request to sit at his right and left in the Kingdom. (Mark 10:35-43)
- Was with Jesus in the Garden of Gethsemane.(Matthew 26:36-46)
- Witnessed the miraculous catch of fish on the Sea of Galilee after Jesus' resurrection. (John 21:2-7)

Stand firm in the face of persecution.

Some claim he was the first bishop in Spain.

Symbols of James sometimes include the bishop's hat and the sword, which is in reference to his martyrdom.

John

- Son of Zebedee
- Boanerges (Son of Thunder)
- "The Beloved Disciple" (The disciple whom Jesus loved)
- "The Evangelist"
- "The Revealer"

- Son of Zebedee. (Matthew 4:21)
- Son of Salome. (Matthew 27:56; Mark 16:1)
- Fisherman with his father and his brother. (Matthew 4:18-22)
- Brother of James. (Matthew 4:21)
- Partner with Peter. (Luke 5:10)
- One of the pillars of the Jerusalem church. (Galatians 2:9)
- Healed and preached. (Acts 3–4; 8)
- Exiled to the island of Patmos. (Revelation 1:1, 9)
- Wrote the Gospel of John, 1, 2, and 3 John, and Revelation.

- Vengeful and fiery. (Luke 9:54)
- Judgmental. (Mark 9:38)
- Selfish. (Mark 10:35-37)
- Bold, loving and compassionate after Pentecost. (Acts 4:13; 1 John 4)

- One of the three disciples in the core group of disciples. (Mark 5:37; 9:2; 13:3; 14:33)
- Suggested that driving out demons could only be performed by those who follow Jesus and his disciples. (Mark 9:38)
- Witnessed Jesus' Transfiguration (where Jesus' divinity was revealed). (Mark 9:2-8)
- Was sent to prepare the upper room for the Last Supper. (Luke 22:8)
- Reclined next to Jesus during the Last Supper. (John 13:23)
- Was given the responsibility at the cross to take care of Mary, Jesus' mother. (John 19:26, 27)
- Ran ahead of Peter to see Jesus' empty tomb and expressed faith by "seeing and believing." (John 20:2-8)
- Witnessed the miraculous catch of fish on the Sea of Galilee after Jesus' resurrection. (John 21:2-7)

God's love, evident in Jesus Christ, saves, transforms, and unites all believers.

Some stories suggest that John was released from exile on the island of Patmos and returned to Ephesus (Turkey today).

Stories suggest that John died in Ephesus around AD 100.

Symbols of John sometimes include the eagle (Revelation 4:7) and a book.

Matthew

- Levi
- Levi the son of Alphaeus

- Son of Alphaeus. (Mark 2:14)
- From Capernaum. (Mark 2:1-17)
- Tax collector in Galilee. (Matthew 9:9)
- Possible brother of James son of Alphaeus. (Mark 3:18)
- Listed as one of Christ's twelve disciples. (Matthew 10:2-4; Acts 1:13)
- Wrote the Gospel of Matthew
- The name Matthew derives from Hebrew, meaning "gift of God."

- Penitent. (Matthew 9:9; 10:2)
- Hospitable. (Matthew 9:10)

- Matthew left his tax collector booth to follow Jesus. (Matthew 9:9)
- Matthew invited Jesus over to dine with him and his corrupt friends. (Matthew 9:10)
- Sent out on a mission to the Jews to preach "the kingdom of heaven is at hand," heal the sick, cleanse the lepers, raise the dead, and cast out demons. (Matthew 10:5-8)
- Was present at the Last Supper (Matthew 26:20)

Jesus Christ is for everyone, even sinners and outcasts.

Some stories suggest that Matthew ministered to Persia, Macedonia, Syria, Parthia, Media, and Ethiopia bringing the good news to kings.

Some stories suggest that Matthew died a martyr.

The symbol for Matthew is sometimes a bag of coins in reference to his occupation as a tax collector before he encountered Jesus.

Thomas

- Didymus (Twin)
- Judas Thomas
- "Doubting Thomas"

- He was a twin. (John 20:24)
- Listed as one of Christ's twelve disciples. (Matthew 10:2-4; Mark 3:16-19; Luke 6:14-16)

- Inquisitive. (John 14:5)
- Doubtful. (John 20:24, 25)
- Courageous. (John 11:16)
- Faithful. (John 20:24-29)

- Courageously encouraged disciples to go to Bethany. (John 11:16)
- Asked Jesus how to know where Jesus was going. (John 14:5)
- Doubted Jesus' resurrection saying he would have to touch his wounds in order to believe. (John 20:25)
- Affirmed that Jesus was Lord and God. (John 20:28)
- Witnessed the miraculous catch of fish and ate breakfast with Jesus after his resurrection. (John 21:2-7)

Jesus can overcome doubts and lead believers to faithfulness.

Stories suggest that Thomas traveled to India and founded the Christian church there.

Some suggest Thomas was killed by a spear for his faith, and was buried in India.

Some say Thomas was a carpenter.

Symbols for Thomas include the spearhead and the T-square.

Philip

- None

- Born in Bethsaida.(John 1:44)
- Well versed in Scripture. (John 1:45, 46)
- Listed as one of Christ's twelve disciples. (Matthew 10:2-4; Mark 3:16-19; Luke 6:14-16)
- The disciple Philip is often confused with Philip the evangelist found in Acts.
- The name Philip derives from Greek, meaning "he who loves horses."
- Philip probably spoke Greek. (John 12:20, 21)

- Practical. (John 6:7)
- Helpful. (John 12:20, 21)
- Literal and confused. (John 14:8)

- The third disciple Jesus called. (John 1:43)
- Brought Nathanael (Bartholomew) to Jesus.(John 1:45, 46)
- Jesus tested him regarding the feeding of the multitude. (John 6:5-7)
- Informed Jesus that several Greeks wanted to see him. (John 12:20-22)
- Asked Jesus to show him the Father. (John 14:8, 9)
- Was present at the Last Supper. (Matthew 26:20)

All the knowledge in the world does not compare to the truth found in Jesus.

Tradition suggests that Philip lived and preached in Scythia (Ukraine today).

Some stories suggest that Philip was crucified on a tall cross at Hierapolis of Phrygia (Turkey today).

Symbols for Philip sometimes include loaves of bread (John 6:5-7) and a tall cross.

Bartholomew

- Nathanael

- Born and/or raised in Cana of Galilee. (John 21:2)
- Well versed in the Hebrew Scriptures. (John 1:46)
- Listed as one of Christ's twelve disciples. (Matthew 10:2-4; Acts 1:13)
- The name Bartholomew derives from Greek, meaning "son of Tolmai."
- The name Nathanael derives from the Hebrew, meaning "God has given."

- Skeptical. (John 1:46)
- Honest. (John 1:47)
- Faithful. (John 1:49)

- Jesus told Nathanael that he was an honest Israelite and informed him that he saw him sitting under the fig tree. (John 1:47, 48)
- Nathanael said that Jesus was the "Son of God" and "King of Israel." (John 1:49)
- Jesus enlightened Nathanael with what to expect (John 1:50, 51)
- Witnessed the miraculous catch of fish and ate breakfast with Jesus after his resurrection. (John 21:2-7)

Believers are called to test all things with Scripture and remain true to its principles.

Some suggest that Bartholomew ministered to Asia Minor and India and the Armenian church claims Bartholomew as their founder.

Tradition suggests that Bartholomew was flayed alive in Armenia.

The symbol for Bartholomew is sometimes a blade.

Andrew

- "Protokletos" (First Called)

- Son of Jona. (John 1:42)
- Born in Bethsaida. (John 1:44)
- Lived in Capernaum with Peter. (Mark 1:29)
- Fisherman. (Matthew. 4:18)
- Brother of Simon Peter. (Matthew 4:18)
- Disciple of John the Baptist.(John 1:35-40)
- Listed as one of Christ's twelve disciples. (Matthew 10:2-4; Mark 3:16-19; Luke 6:14-16)
- The name Andrew derives from Greek, meaning "manly."

- Enthusiastic about Christ. (John 1:35-42)
- Inquisitive. (John 1:35-38)
- Resourceful. (John 6:8, 9)

- First to follow Jesus. (John 1:35-40)
- Called to be a fisher of men. (Matthew 4:19)
- Sent out on a mission to the Jews to preach "the kingdom of heaven is at hand," heal the sick, cleanse the lepers, raise the dead, and cast out demons. (Matthew 10:5-8)
- Informed Jesus that several Greeks wanted to see him. (John 12:20-22)
- Told Jesus of the boy with five loaves of bread and two fish. (John 6:8, 9)
- Was present when Jesus appeared to the disciples after the Resurrection. (John 20:19-25)
- Was present for the Great Commission when Jesus sent his disciples to all nations. (Matthew 28:16-20)
- Witnessed Jesus being taken up into heaven. (Acts 1:8, 9)

Go out and eagerly share the good news about Jesus Christ.

Some suggest that Andrew preached in Greece, Asia Minor, and Russia.
A seventh-century story suggests that Andrew was crucified on an X-shaped cross by a Roman proconsul.
The symbol for Andrew is sometimes the X-shaped cross.

Other Disciples in the New Testament

Other Disciples of Jesus	Apostles, Evangelists and Teachers	Important Leaders
Cleopas: Disciple of Jesus who spoke with Jesus on the road to Emmaus. (Luke 24:18)	**Apollos:** Missionary. (Acts 18:18-27; 1 Corinthians 1:12; 3:4-6, 22; 4:6; 16:12; Titus 3:13)	**Ananias:** Disciple and healer. (Acts 9:11)
James: Brother of Jesus, leader of Jerusalem church, and author of James. (Matthew 13:55, 56; Acts 12:17)	**Aquila:** Teacher and missionary. (Acts 18; Romans 16:3; 1 Corinthians 16:19; 2 Timothy 4:19)	**Archippus:** Leader of house church. (Colossians 4:17; Philemon 2)
Joanna: Disciple of Jesus. (Luke 8:3; 24:10)	**Barnabas:** Missionary, apostle, and partner with Paul. (Acts 4:36; 9–15; 1 Cor. 9:6; Gal. 2:1, 9, 13; Col. 4:10)	**Aristarchus:** Missionary and fellow prisoner with Paul. (Acts19:29; 20:4; 27:2; Colossians 4:10; Philemon 24)
Joseph of Arimathea: Disciple of Jesus. (Matthew 27:57; John 19:38)	**Junia:** Apostle. (Romans 16:7)	**Epaphras:** Preacher, fellow worker and prisoner with Paul. (Colossians 1:7; 4;12; Philemon 23)
Joseph Barsabbas: Disciple of Jesus. (Acts 1:23)	**Luke:** Physician, worker, and prisoner with Paul, and author of Luke. (Colossians 4:14; 2 Timothy 4:11)	**Epaphroditus:** Fellow worker with Paul. (Philippians 2:25; 4:18)
Judas (Jude): Brother of Jesus and author of the book of Jude. (Matthew 13:54, 55; Mark 6:3; Jude 1)	**Mark (John Mark):** Missionary, cousin to Barnabas, and author of the Gospel Mark. (Acts 12; 1 Peter 5:13)	**Judas Barsabbas:** Prophet. (Acts 15:22-35)
Lazarus: Friend and disciple of Jesus. (John 11–12)	**Paul (Saul):** Apostle, missionary, and author of Romans to Philemon. (Acts to Philemon; 2 Peter 3:15)	**Lucius of Cyrene:** Prophet and teacher in the church at Antioch. (Acts 13:1)
Mary, the mother of James and Joseph: Disciple of Jesus. (Matthew 27:55; 28:5, 7)	**Philip the Evangelist:** Deacon and missionary. (Acts 6:5; 8)	**Manaen:** Prophet and teacher of the church in Antioch. (Acts 13:1)
Mary of Bethany: Friend and disciple of Jesus. (Luke 10:38-42; John 11–12)	**Priscilla:** Teacher and missionary. (Acts 18; Romans 16:3; 1 Corinthians 16:19; 2 Timothy 4:19)	**Mnason:** An early disciple. (Acts 21:16)
Mary Magdalene: Disciple of Jesus. (Matthew 27, 28; Mark 15, 16; Luke 8:2; 24:10; John 20)	**Silas:** Missionary. (Acts 15–18; 2 Corinthians 1:19; 1 Thessalonians 1:1; 2 Thessalonians 1:1; 1 Peter 5:12)	**Philemon:** Leader of a house church. (Philemon 1)
Matthias: Disciple who replaced Judas Iscariot. (Acts 1:15-26)	**Stephen:** Deacon, missionary, preacher, and martyr. (Acts 6–8; 11:19; 22:20)	**Phoebe:** Deacon and helper of Paul. (Romans 16:1, 2)
Salome: Disciple of Jesus. (Mark 15:40)	**Timothy:** Pastor and teacher. (Acts 16–20; Rom. 16:21; 1 Cor. 4:17; Philippians 2:19-22; 1 and 2 Timothy)	**Simeon (Niger):** Prophet and teacher in the church at Antioch. (Acts 13:1)
Susanna: Disciple of Jesus. (Luke 8:3)	**Titus:** Pastor and teacher. (2 Corinthians 2:13; 7:6; 8:6-23; 12:18; Galatians. 2:1-3; Titus 1:4, 5)	**Tychicus:** Pastor and fellow worker with Paul. (Ephesians 6:21; Colossians 4:7)

Being a Disciple of Christ

Beginning the Journey: Count the Cost

- Jesus said that whoever wants to follow him, that person must deny himself and take up his cross. He said that if one wants to save his life he will lose it, but if he loses his life for Jesus and for the gospel he will save it.
- When Simon Peter, James and John encountered Jesus, they pulled their boats up on shore, left everything and followed him.

Following Christ Together: Fellowship

- Jesus prayed that his followers would be brought to complete unity.
- The followers of Jesus were not to give up meeting together and were to encourage one another.

Serving Christ and Others

- Jesus said that whoever wants to become great among his disciples must be a servant, just as Jesus himself did not come to be served, but to serve, and "to give his life a ransom for many."

Failures and Forgiveness

- When Jesus was arrested all the disciples deserted him and fled, and Peter denied knowing him because he feared for his life.
- Later Jesus said that the disciples would receive power when the Holy Spirit came to them and that they would share the good news in Jerusalem, and in all Judea and Samaria, and all over the earth.

In the Power of the Spirit

- Jesus promised the disciples that he would send the Holy Spirit to them, and that the Holy Spirit would guide them and provide them with gifts that would help them carry out their mission.
- Paul wrote to the Corinthian church informing them that there is only one Spirit, but different kinds of gifts. There is only one God, but several kinds of good works.

(Mark 8:34, 35; Luke 5:11b; John 17:23a; Hebrews 10:25; Matthew 20:26-28; Matthew 26:56b; Mark 14:71, 72; Acts 1:8; John 16:5-16; 1 Corinthians 12:4-12)

ROSE PUBLISHING

Published by Rose Publishing
an imprint of Tyndale House Ministries

rose-publishing.com

Art for the disciples was selected from art produced by selected Renaissance masters including Tiziano Vecellio (Titian) and Jacopo Robusti (Tintoretto).

ISBN 978-1-89094-793-4

9 781890 947934

471X *The Twelve Disciples*

Other Names

General Information

Personality & Character

Encounters with Jesus

Key Lesson

Stories